All Scripture references taken from the KJV of the Bible unless otherwise indicated.

Level the Playing Field, by Dr. Marlene Miles

Freshwater Press 2023

ISBN: 978-1-960150-76-9

Copyright 2023 by Dr. Marlene Miles

All rights reserved. No part of this book may be reproduced, distributed or transmitted by any means or in any means including photocopying, recording or other electronic or mechanical methods without prior written permission of the publisher except in the case of brief publications or critical reviews.

Table of Contents

The Playing Field 4
Am I Cursed? 11
The Player's Field 20
Level This Field, *Already*! 25
Heal Your Foundation 35
Oh, That Flesh Life 44
First Things First 48
It Is Good to Repent 58
Outside of Time 60
Prayer Is Not a Question 62
What Did You Say? 65
A Thousand May Fall 70
A Field Like *Theirs*? 76
What Are You *Even* Asking For? 78
Favor Is Not Fair 82
Heal My Foundation Prayer 84
Other books by this author 104

Level the Playing Field

Freshwater Press

The Playing Field

> These are murmurers complainers walking after their own lusts and their mouth speaketh great swelling words having men's persons in admiration because of advantage.
>
> (Jude 1:16)

So many people complain that the "playing field" is not level. They say that some people have *privilege*, and even major advantages over others. We know who is complaining--, not the people who seem to have the advantage. Those with eyes to see, see good things happening for others and not for themselves. They see good things happening in other families, but not in their own. It may even be happening for the family across the street, or across town, but not for them--, not for their family. They see successes happening for a grandfather, a father and a son--, generation after generation, in a certain family, but again, not theirs.

Humans notice the **obvious and sometimes do not look any further, or any deeper.** What do *they*--, these successful people and families who have advantages, and a great life, look like? What is different about them? What kind of house do *they* live in? What car or cars do they have? What's their job? We most immediately surmise they are blessed because *they* have **money**.

Well, this is the conclusion we reach if we are money-focused, or money-driven. If we are *other* focused, say education focused, we might believe that a certain family is successful because they all went to college. What we see at any time depends on our own *filters,* what we've been through in life and what we expect to happen in life.

We do need money to survive, to conduct our flesh lives and take care of the flesh body that we are using right now. Remember, we are not only flesh; we should be conducting our **entire** life, not just our flesh life. The Word even says that money answers all things, (Eccl 10:19) but we still are so much more than just flesh.

Contrary to a lot of worldly teaching, being money-focused will not solve the unlevel playing field issue because unfair advantages and unlevel playing fields are really a thing. But many complain as if the field that they can't get on or win on is made entirely *of* **money**.

Still, as we look, and not wanting to be or appear bitter, we may look at all *they* have. Celebrities, stars, athletes, and top businessmen, and the people who live on the *good* side of the tracks--, what they have, or appear to have *is* **money**, as far as we know, as far as we can see, that is what we notice – the obvious.

We may take a look at what is missing or could be missing from *their* lives because *their* lives are just a little bit of our concern, right now. We need to pay attention to what **_we_** are supposed to be doing about our own lives. If we are *they*-focused, or *them*-focused, that will not solve the irregular playing field, either. Lots of people work and play on fields, seemingly full of money, and they still have issues – human issues, things that are common to all people. Emotional issues, mental issues, relationship issues, issues with their children, and health issues. Yeah, money helps in some matters, but not in everything.

Do these fortunate looking people have spiritual issues? Many do. We see reports of confused spirituality and disastrous practices that famous and not-so-famous people do, for success and for money.

Money is the **_cause_** of some issues; after all, the lust for it is the root of all evil.

Really, what we want to know is why isn't our own life working out? Why don't great things happen to *us*? Why don't people help **us** get from Point A to Point B? When will *we* get a break? Why isn't this field *level*? Why does that guy make twice the amount of money you make, and you work at the *same* job doing the same thing?

We, too often, conclude that it is because the **playing field** is not level.

In reality--, it's not. **The playing field is not level.** Even though in this country the Constitution says that *"All men are created equal."* All playing fields are not created equal, but playing fields **are** created.

Even if the playing field is not level, looking to another man to solve field disparity is inadequate. Man, either *won't* do it, can't do it, or can only do it to some degree, if he is even willing. Whether or not he, you, or the two of you together or with others can make this field level, depends on who *you* are, and who you are to God.

The average unsaved man won't put you as his equal or higher than himself because he's merely a man. Therefore, you, you, **you** have a big role to play in tamping this playing field to *level*. I won't quote the bootstraps saying because it makes no sense to me, but if the field you are either born onto, or find yourself on is not level, then that means that **you** have work to do.

Even if a good-hearted, natural man comes into your life to try to help you, he can't go past *who you are spiritually*, even if that man is in God and spiritual himself, he can't go past where **spiritual forces** allow him to go in order to help you. No matter how badly you need or even want him to help you in life, these are natural solutions. **The playing field is spiritual**. You can throw every natural solution you can think of at a spiritual problem, and the problem will persist.

You just want to be treated equally, live in a good house and drive a nice car with money for your expenses, *right*? While some don't want you to get ahead of them in life, some don't want you to get ahead of where you even started out in life, because playing field issues are spiritual.

I'm not talking about those people right now. I'm talking about decent people who are helpful, who do what they can do to make things right in this world; the rest is on you.

That natural man, aside from not wanting to lose his high or top position, may **not** be able to assist you to get where you want to be, from where you are. It could be the old, *you can't get there from here* problem.

Sometimes.

Perhaps we mistakenly think that *they* own the field—, all the fields, or all the playing fields, and *by golly*, they should share. There is some murmuring and complaining going on here and that will get you *what*? Pretty much nothing. Oh, you just want to vent because *they* have all the advantages.

Last I saw, the Earth is the Lord's and the fulness thereof. Actually, Psalm 115 says God gave Earth to man, and if you're a man and of mankind, then there is some Earth that you should be **owning**.

The heaven, even the heavens, are the LORD's:
But the earth hath he given to the children of men.
(Psalm 115:16)

God has given Earth to man. You're a man. Are you *in God*? Then you can expect the promises of God to come to you; there is some <u>earth</u>--, *some part of this Earth is* **<u>for you</u>**. There is a field for you.

You must be *in* God to know where it is and to get it.

Trust that if God has a *field* for you, it is custom made for you; and **you** will do very well, or even dominate on that field.

Until we know that, we will be looking at other people, what they have and how they are dominating ***the field.*** In noticing this we may be calling that field **unlevel,** in our murmuring and complaining.

Am I Cursed?

I was talking with a man recently who asked me if I thought he was cursed or living a cursed life. If any of us are living under curses we need to know it, so we can do something about it. Saints of God, we only have to look in the Bible to see what the curses are (Deuteronomy 28, *et. al.*). We check off the ones that are happening in our life. Even if it's only one, that is still living under the Curse of the Law.

First, are you saved?

The curses are: sickness, poverty and death. If you're *not* saved, you are living under the Curse of the Law no matter what it looks like in the natural. You could **be saved** and still be living under a curse if you don't realize it and are not proactive to do something about it.

If you are cursed or living under a curse or curses, you *will* be treated differently by **everyday people** than that guy who isn't living under a curse. Why? It's spiritual, and it's a law. It's the Law of

Sin & Death. If you sin, or are a sinner, then ***death*** is the result, either quickly or slowly. On the way to death is sickness and poverty in any of their manifestations.

Are you under a curse? Discriminated against? Reproached? Are you being hated for no reason, it seems? Have you fallen from favor? Are you being disrespected? The word, *curse* is mentioned nearly 200 times in the Bible; so, curses are real.

How you are being treated may not even be your fault, it could be generational on either side of your family. It could be generational on either side of the *discrimination*, if that is what is happening to you. There could be a *spirit of reproach, or rejection* or a *spirit of hatred* on you.

Or the person doing the discriminating could be operating under an altar of lies, where they believe lies about you or people *like you*—, tall people short people--, whatever your description is. Or they could be functioning under an altar of false accusations (against you, old people, young people, --people *like* you), or both things could be happening. A compound issue means *you* have to be doubly aware of it, be saved, or get saved, and be ready to do something, *spiritually* about it.

You may be thinking, well, I'm a human being, he doesn't have to treat me like that.

Yes, he does; it is spiritual. If he doesn't treat you *like that*, the devil will find other people who will treat you *like that*. It will happen. If you have these *spirits* on you or in you--, you will be treated the way that matches those *spirits*, until you do something about it–, spiritually. Further, the *spirits* that are in him will cause him to behave or misbehave in a certain way.

If we know nothing else, it is that we cannot solve spiritual problems with natural solutions. Wishing, hoping, murmuring, complaining, trying harder, assimilating, trying to fit in--, those are natural things, flesh things; if the problem is spiritual, it must be solved **spiritually**.

You know you haven't done anything to this person or these people who may be hating on you, seeming to hold you back, or hindering your progress and success. And you probably haven't. Could be that you inherited it. No, not that they knew your ancestors and have a beef with them, necessarily, although there are famous long-standing family feuds. No, they inherited the *spirit* of it.

Chad is sure that he doesn't have a racist bone in his body, but he *inherited* that hate. The *spirits* that are in him will make him act out, even if he doesn't want to, or isn't planning to. Whatever you worship, or whatever **comes with** what you worship, you become like that thing, even if it is an idol *god*, or a demon. If Chad is clueless spiritually and his victim is also clueless, spiritually, what will either of them do to solve the problem? If they try to solve it at all, they will only do flesh, obvious things.

The playing field is not level, but it appears that Chad has the advantage. Chad is dominating, like he owns this *field*; but does he?

No, God gave Earth to man--, not just Chad.

If Chad is winning, unsaved and unspiritual, he may not see that there is a problem here, even if you are telling him. Even if you are protesting, demonstrating, yelling--, he either can't hear you, or sees no need in hearing you.

You need God. Will the problems in your life finally drive you to God? Or, is this not rock-bottom enough?

If unspiritual Chad does nothing to help, that means **you** have all the work to do, you have to handle this--, spiritually. We don't war with flesh and blood; we aren't going to fight with Chad.

But the question you need to ask yourself is: *Am I cursed,* or is **the man** just treating me badly? Is **the man** treating me badly because I'm cursed?

Outside of being saved, you may not have a way to either pose, or answer this question, so you may need someone to help you, tell you, and teach you. You will definitely need Jesus. You need Jesus to save you if you want to be delivered from playing field issues, which are the sequela to curses, **stay delivered and have a victorious life.**

A curse is a barrier that keeps a person from the good things, the promises of God. A curse can be uttered by any person, not just a witch or wizard. There are *blind witches*, well-meaning people like parents, friends, who say things they shouldn't that the devil can twist into curses unbeknownst to them. Who are we kidding? There are husbands and wives who argue and say horrible things to each other that are curses; they speak words that should never come out of their mouths.

Automatically, the curse comes when sin is committed and not repented of.

A curse is the spell that is cast on a person, a family, or a group. There are family curses. There can be **territorial** curses, such as a neighborhood curse. Curses allow a principality or strongman to be over an area to enforce the curse. Bad things happen in an area no matter how hard people try to make good things happen there. Certain things cannot happen for people in a territory, for example, no matter what they try.

A land could be cursed and needs to be redeemed. Every place is not necessarily cursed, but the devil is the prince of this world and has set up ruling, spiritual principalities all over the world. An area, a neighborhood, a house could be under a curse, and just by virtue of walking into that area, territory, live in that territory, or house, or try to work in it, the curse affects you negatively.

It's like walking out in the rain; you get wet.

The curse on that territory makes the playing field of that area, you guessed it--, **unlevel**. Curses need to be dealt with spiritually, for individuals. When a curse is over an area sometimes your warfare has to include praying and fasting, as Daniel had to do in the Book of Daniel. That area curse may not even be against you specifically, but it involves you now, so you have authority if you're saved, to pray and do something about it. To make sure your prayers are being heard when praying about an area, territory, business, a house that concerns you, you have to be sure **you** have authority to pray about the matter that you are addressing. If you don't, your prayers will not be heard; the heavens will be shut up against you. We'll go more into this later.

There are as many different reasons as to why the playing field is not level as there are **spiritual interferences** in an area, a territory, a state or a country--, or in an individual's or family's foundation. Some of these interferences are long term, inherited, fully embedded strongmen or principalities. Some devils were just sent out yesterday by some witch, maybe *Sharon*, whom I'll tell you about later, or someone else you don't even know who hates you for whatever reason.

Territorial spirits/strongmen make the playing field unlevel in entire areas, states, regions, countries. Are you even supposed to be *there*? How did you happen to come to be there or live there?

There are some places demons want **no** humans–, some shrines, "churches", historical places, for example. The territory, the Earth itself could be against you – it's why we don't war against humans, it may not be the humans that are against you. It may *look* as though humans are against you because that is their spiritual assignment, and wouldn't the devil want to make mankind hate one another and fight one another? If a person is unsaved, clueless, occultic, or demonic, they will be doing, clueless, occultic, or demonic things, as if on remote.

This is probably why Jesus said, **"Lord, forgive them, for they know not what they do."**

Curses stop progress and successes. They stop people. Cursed people struggle a lot and are often frustrated and disappointed, sent back to square zero, when they thought they were making progress.

In your life or family do you see poverty, sickness, untimely deaths, haters, mental illness, accidents, family strife and discord--, the family just can't get along? Are there late marriages, no marriages, barrenness, unfruitful wombs, nightmares, night terrors, *spirit spouse*, strange battles, weird obstacles, divorces? If you encounter frustration even when trying to accomplish simple things, you could be under a curse or curses, of the family, ancestral, generational and/or territorial variety.

Chad--, yeah, him again. Chad looks like he's dominating the field, but *is he*? Not really because if Chad is not spiritual, **the spiritual stuff is dominating**. The curse is dominating; spiritual things unopposed, unanswered are very powerful. Positive or negative, if it is unopposed, it will dominate. The curse unopposed is running the *field* and running all over certain players on that field--, those who are susceptible. Ask yourself, *Am I cursed?* If you are, then you are susceptible. What am I talking about? There are whole countries that are war-ridden; as soon as one war is over, another starts. *Is that country's "playing field" level?*

In your particular case, you must ask God. Get saved if you are not and then ask God.

But, as long as your eyes are on *Chad*, either because you're bitter, thinking he's privileged, or you want to hob nob with him because you think he will help you get ahead, or because of jealousy, you secretly want to undermine him, when will you *ever* see God? When will you ever seek God?

The Player's Field

You believe that you're a good guy, but you may not understand why **women** don't *know their place*. Why can't they just be cool, like guys--, what's wrong with them? Those women--, just because you spent some time with them, doesn't mean you're obligated to date or marry them. If you're saved, it does; you don't lead people on, especially women. You also don't waste people's time.

If you're unsaved – well, Hell is already making reservations for people who think like that.

We all need Jesus! Women are not toys.

And there you are discriminating against women. Can you not see that what you're doing to a certain woman, or to women, in general, is what you think or say that Chad is doing to *you*. But you justify it by saying you're a man, and you're just *playing the field*.

The field?

What *field*? Really--, the field?

Is the ***field*** that you want to play on the same for men and women, while you're murmuring and complaining that a professional or career field is not level for you? How about for gender? How about for people of different ages? *Is it the same?* God does not like hypocrites.

There is no male and female in God, but if **you're** not *in* God, **AND also** spiritual, when will you see this? The male-female field is not level either, *is it?*

So, this lady, let's call her Sharon, also sees that the field is not level and she, like you, hates it. How have you treated Sharon? --Not good.

Sharon, who is also unsaved, thinks her brand of *spirituality* will solve this problem because she's tired of meeting and dating "dogs," and old dudes, because that is who is checking for her these days. Sharon hates old people, but she can't see how *she's* being a hypocrite, either.

Anyway, she's teed off at you right now, so she starts into some dark arts--, her kind of "*spirituality*" which is totally ungodly. Then you, a victim already, will attract **more** curses to you because Sharon is spitting them out, she's sending them out against you and you're a sinner. It's so easy – curses will stick automatically when you're in disobedience and sin.

Sharon hates you now and wishes bad things for your life, she wishes bad things for your money and relationships. More hatred, more delays, more reproach, more near-success syndrome, more diversion of blessings and even *evil exchange* are coming your way.

I know more than one person who shared a great invention idea with folks they know who stole their ideas completely. They became successful and the person who had the original idea got nothing. People steal all the time. People who are under a curse are easy to steal from, both in the natural and spiritually, more so than people who are *in* the Kingdom and have God's protection.

You and Sharon seem to be aware that there are problems in your respective lives, but if you think the problem is money or privilege, or related to either, you will try to solve the problem without removing the **cause** of the problem. The cause of the problem is sin; it always is. It is either hers or yours, your ancestors, your sins, your iniquity. And, for her--, *hers*. Sins that are not repented for have iniquity. Iniquity passes down through generations.

As spirits, we should realize that the natural manifestation we see is not the problem, the problem is a **spiritual** issue that eventually shows up in the natural to alert us, torment us, or worse. Demons (devils) come to steal, kill and destroy. With our natural minds we can't even correctly determine what the problem is if it is a spiritual problem and as I've said, it most often is.

Chad, on the other hand, doesn't think he has a problem, even though there are serious medical patterns that run in his family. On the surface, and right now, things are all in his favor. If Chad is carnal, not saved, living his flesh life, he believes that's all there is, and he has *arrived*. But there are demons in Chad's foundation assigned to trouble him and his health, in the future.

After mistreating Sharon, your problems may get worse because of Sharon's shenanigans. Sharon's problems will worsen because of the idol *gods* (demons) that she is calling on to do bad stuff to you because you didn't treat her well. Sharon doesn't think she's calling on demons, she thinks she is a *chosen one* who can talk to *spirits*, *spirit guides*, angels, and the like. She is deceived, not having considered what "angels" she is speaking to. Angels are either from God, or from the devil.

There are no neutral angels without spiritual designation waiting for man to "program" them. Sharon is talking to *familiar spirits, guardian demons* and devils masquerading as being sent from God. They are not. How do I know this? If you did not go to God, by way of Jesus Christ, the "angels" dispatched are default to this Earth, they are of the devil. They are fallen angels, emissaries of the prince of this world. They are demons.

Sharon is not aware of the covering cast over her life that is blocking her from her Kingdom husband. And, she's not aware of the *rejection* and *reproach* that is on her because of her sin and her hateful and vengeful ways. This causes the men she dates, while trying to find the right one, to treat her well at first, and then disappear. Like you did. She can't see this because she is not saved, angry, and deeply involved in the occult.

Like you, Sharon cannot attract a Kingdom spouse because she is unsaved, and not in the Kingdom, although we all want God's stuff. We want God's best. But we need to be *in* God to get all of the promises He has for us.

Level This Field, *Already*!

In order to have a level field, your foundation must be level. The **Earth** under your foundation has to be working *for* you and not against you. (More on that later.)

But right now, who builds a house on a warped foundation? You can't build anything on a bad foundation; it won't stand. A level field in sports means that both players have equal opportunity to get the ball and run with it to score. I'm using this term to mean that the *field* needs to be level for **you**, so you can build on it as you build your life. I do not mean that your field should equal to or be in competition with Chad. God is the standard, not Chad.

Dear Reader, I may mention other foundations, but primarily you should be most concerned about one foundation – **yours**.

This is not about competing with others or comparing yourself with others, although it is natural to notice that to get from Point A to Point B takes 1 month, but in 3 years you haven't gotten there yet. But Chad has. Sharon, in 4 years hasn't gotten there, but you don't care about her, she's *only a woman*. Furthermore, she's behind you, so if you're unsaved, you don't really care-, but you want other unsaved people to care about you. Isn't this the same thing you're accusing Chad of?

Chad is not the reason you're not at your point of breakthrough or success; your **foundation** is the reason. Chad is not the reason your playing field is not level; <u>**your** **foundation is the reason**</u>. Chad is also not the person to help you get there or make sure you get there, unless Chad is your parent, a destiny helper, or a qualified person to move Earth. (In this case, he is not.)

My point is, if *your* foundation is not even level, how will you play in the game of life, and be successful? We seem to worry more about playing fields because that surface stuff, it is the most obvious.

Chad is not responsible for your foundation. The foundation is **spiritual**. Your *spiritual* foundation is the compilation of all the spiritual things that have been invited or allowed into your ancestral background, that has not been repented of, dealt with, and gotten rid of, substituting it with only Godly things. If we want Godly results, conditions, and situations for our lives, we must be that. Allow that. Only allow that; and reject everything that is not Godly. This is like wanting symptoms to go away, but not getting rid of the **problem** that causes the symptoms.

Wanting what God has without God is not sustainable.

Yes, Chad made it—, he is successful. We can take lessons and inspiration from winners, but looking to a man because he's got it going on in the natural, without looking any deeper at *this man*, is not how we get promoted in life. That's brown nosing, idolatry.

The man you're supposed to look the deepest at is **you**. Are you saved? Are you living under a curse or curses? Is your *playing field* helping you, or hindering you?

Promotion comes from God. That's where we should be looking. God is the Author and the Finisher of our faith. Every time we or any of our ancestors have ignored God, bypassed God and sought some other *spirit, power,* or *entity* for help, success, money, protection--, anything, we've polluted our lives, upset our playing field, and in the long term, corrupted the foundations of our bloodline.

We are **spirits**. Our flesh lives in time and space, but our spirits are not limited to time and space.

Our foundation is spiritual. What's in your foundation was put there or allowed to be there, spiritually, by your parents and ancestors, and you. What did they leave you? It's not just about what they left you financially or physically, but what they left you, *spiritually*.

When we find a faulty ancestral foundation, we are in for horrible surprises as we peel back the **causes** to our life's problems, one layer at a time, providing we look that deeply. We must stay spiritual and not go into the flesh in order to do this. If we are bitter, blaming others, we won't look. If we are jealous, envious of others, we won't look. If we are competitive against flesh and blood, we will never look for the cause. If we only want relief, to fix the symptoms of the problem, or get the results a person or a people group with a *different* foundation may be getting, we may get careless or desperate and make bad choices.

Prayers abound for the healing of one's foundation. That healing occurs when you get everything out of your foundation that is not of God, no matter how it got there. Once saved; you are a new creation in Christ and now in the family of God. By your being adopted into the Kingdom, you are adopted into a new bloodline--, that of Christ. After all, if you are saved your spirit is regenerated and you work out your salvation by renewing your mind, which is in your soul. You don't just get saved and do nothing else.

Sometimes we won't know what was left to us, spiritually, from our father's house, in our foundation until natural problems show up. The wiser man or woman of God seeks to detect problems as early as possible--, when they are spiritual problems, in order to pray and block them from becoming natural problems that are so much harder to get rid of.

But Chad--, *what about Chad?* Chad's foundation must have been pretty good as far as education and finances go. He went to college, made great grades, graduated and got a position in the same company where you work. He got promoted, quickly, but you didn't.

You're still trying to go to college, part-time, paying your own way because your parents can't afford tuition. Worse than that, your parents are struggling, so you sit out semesters at a time from college, and work to try to help your folks. Lack of an educational degree is why you didn't get promoted, but Chad did.

I am in no way saying do not help your parents; you should honor father and mother. But, a backward altar is working against you if you're paying for your *past* right now instead of your present, or preparing for your future. That is a sign of a backward pull on your life; it is a foundational problem. As you try to correct spiritual issues from your known or unknown **ancestors,** in so doing **you're trying to correct spiritual issues** with natural solutions.

The ancestors created a spiritual problem which affects the family's finances, so you work more, get two jobs, three jobs, don't go to school, but work in order to get money to give to your parents to throw at this spiritual problem. Being money focused, many think that throwing money at a thing will solve that thing. Because of this *work a thousand jobs* idea of yours, your education is stalled, stunted, or stopped completely.

Somehow, somewhere down your bloodline someone or some one*s* made a covenant with idol *gods (demons)—possibly involving money.* Families that have the **exact same money problem** generation after generation are under a foundational curse where an ancestor made a devil-deal and did not fulfill it because they couldn't, and they did not repent and seek God concerning it. Most often, what you sin with is what the devil is allowed to touch in your life.

Now these demons are interfering with your life because the evil covenant your ancestor created involved your entire bloodline. Whether you stop college or not, whether you get three jobs or five jobs, these problems will still happen until spiritual problems are dealt with, ***spiritually***, all the way down to their root cause. Even though your ancestors are long gone, they hindered your parents' lives, and prosperity. Now, tag--, you're it.

These demons have legal rights to tamper with your life and will assert their rights against you until you get **saved, get spiritual, get knowledge and Wisdom and the Holy Spirit and start praying.** It will persist or worsen until you do something about it. Get deliverance.

You must level the playing field, *spiritually,* before you see a change in your situation and condition in the natural world.

Why are these idol *gods (demons)* messing with you? You don't know them, you don't know anything about them (necessarily), and you are not *worshipping* them. And that is where the problem is: they want **worship**; they want **sacrifice**. They don't usually want money; but they will mess with your money, health--, anything. They really want **blood**, so this is nothing to play with. If they don't get what they want or think they are owed, they usually take it. Demons tormenting, stealing from humans, and also killing, is what curses look like in the natural. They come to steal, kill and destroy. When you see Sharon, who right now thinks she is talking with *angels* or powerful "beings" in her occultic practices, be sure to tell her this.

When these demonic attacks are going on, sometimes it seems there is nothing a human victim can do about it. There isn't –, **without Jesus.** We all need Jesus.

Obviously, a cursed foundation and an uncursed foundation are two entirely different things. Chad's foundation seems pretty **level,** whereas your foundation is bumpy, and/or a total uphill climb, that is, if you are doing it all in the flesh. You don't even know what your ancestors did – or who they even are! This is how people, even people who we think are good people, live defeated lives. **Spiritual *things* are battling them**, but they either don't believe in that *stuff,* or they are ignorant as to what to do about it, so they struggle relentlessly, in the flesh.

In the flesh, those who lean on their own understanding seek to solve this in their own ways. Often, it's the star child of the family, the smart one is tapped to *save* the family by becoming educated and working a good job or getting a high paying professional career. The pretty child of the family is the hope to *save* the family by being *discovered* as a model or an actor, make lots of money and save the family. The talented child of the family is tagged to save the family by getting some lucrative career with their talents such as music or sports.

Jesus saves. Only Jesus. We all need Him.

Often times this is all happening while the spiritual child of the family and his or her Wisdom is largely ignored by the family. Yet, the spiritual one in a family has Godly Wisdom that will heal this family, this foundation, and level the family playing field.

How will one person *save* an entire family, in the flesh? How can one person heal the lifetime issues of his family **bloodline**, especially not really knowing what the issues are? How will one person do this in *one* lifetime? Sadly, except for the spiritual child, the entire family is working from the same faulty foundation. The Godly child who is spiritual has prayed, sought deliverance, and allowed the Lord to heal their foundation. In so doing the Godly and spiritual child is living life on a playing field that is not against him or her.

You need Jesus. We all need Jesus. It is the only way this can be done. We need to heal our foundation; Jesus can do that. Jesus is that One.

Heal Your Foundation

If the foundations be destroyed what shall the righteous do? If a bloodline's foundation is destroyed, damaged, polluted or corrupted, what shall that family do? We know the answer is not to send out one child or even all the children in a family to *save* the family from the depths of despair and poverty, or whatever woes plague that family. Even if every child is successful financially, money is not the only thing that is needed to heal a foundation.

Genesis sets forth the foundation for man to be able to live on this planet and be successful. When parents have a child, they create a nursery for their baby to come home to, *right*? `The Earth is the giant nursery that God created for all of mankind, but He doesn't expect us to stay as babies. Some things we must do ourselves; we can't get Chad or anyone else to do it for us. We don't look to the privileged, the powerful, or the wealthy to do for us what we should be getting from God. Men are not God.

We take sustenance, life, our being and victories from the Mighty Hand of God.

> In the beginning God created the heavens and the earth. Now the earth was formless and void, and darkness was over the surface of the deep. And the Spirit of God was hovering over the surface of the waters. And God said, Let there be light. (Genesis 1:1-3)

On the Second Day God continued to set order. He built everything--, waters, skies, and *et cetera*, and put living things in all of it. In spite of all that building, speaking, ordering, organizing, and creating, in Genesis, by Chapter 3 man had sinned and ruined all of it.

God kept saying, ***It is good***, when He was creating. When He was organizing and creating, He said more than once, ***It is good***. But one sinner can destroy a lot of good. Adam & Eve, two sinners –, all the more ruining God's creation and plan for mankind. Adam & Eve killed it, and not in a good way.

Your ancestors, or maybe only one ancestor could have ruined the whole thing for your family. We don't know who, we don't know when, we don't even know why or what they did unless the Holy Spirit tells us. We just know that if the foundation of our life is jacked, we'd better do something about it, *spiritually*. The foundation that leads to the *field* you are trying to have a successful life on, is not level.

For example, like Sharon, there are women who keep meeting the same kind of man, no matter what you call him, a dog, creep, jerk--, he is the wrong kind of man. **THIS IS A FOUNDATION PROBLEM.** Man or woman, if you keep meeting the exact same wrong person as a suitor or possible spouse, this is a foundation problem–, *your* foundation's problem. Your job is not to fix him, ladies; fix <u>**you**</u>. Let Jesus fix your foundation.

Invoking idol *gods* for revenge is not the solution. We need our foundations healed; we need Jesus.

Everything God made is alive. God doesn't make anything dead. When He rolls up on something dead, He *quickens* it to make it alive, therefore it lives. You need Jesus; we all do. *That* God doesn't make anything dead is why He is so repulsed by dead, fake, idol *gods*. Dead works. Dead faith. Spiritless dry bones. Dead humans.

Looking on the heart of man, God clearly sees if a man is spiritually alive or spiritually dead; He even takes His Spirit from the *dead* that are yet walking.

If you have not accepted Jesus as your Lord and Savior and invited Him to sit on the Throne of your heart, or if you are bound up in sin, then you are *spiritually* dead. Yes, walking the Earth, but dead, spiritually. It doesn't matter if you get on a playing field or not, especially if you plan to accomplish everything in your flesh, you won't be very successful, even in an entire lifetime.

We need Jesus.

Being dead, you will attract and be attractive to dead things--, such as *idols, demons & flies*. Dead things will appeal to you and even if they don't, you will have little to no ability to resist them. Dead things. Dead ideas. More sins. If you're dead, that's your level. You will most likely be attracted to other spiritually dead people, that is what will draw you. We all need Jesus, or we will stay dead; even if we are still breathing and vertical, some days.

The only way to become **undead** is to accept Jesus on this side of physical death. After the physical body dies, there's no more opportunity to be *quickened*, and made spiritually alive, in Christ.

When you invite Jesus into your life, He will quicken you, as in a resuscitation, with Holy Ghost heart paddles – CLEAR!, and then you will live. Amen. Once alive, you will start to classify dead things as dead, and not as options for your life anymore. This keeps your field <u>level</u>. You don't create problems and curses that make bumps and wrinkles that interrupt the incline and topography of the *field* of your life, because these things will not be able to stick to you or your foundation.

Once alive, you won't look at dead things as an option for food, entertainment, a date, or a spouse.

It's like going to a restaurant that creates delicious fresh dishes versus one that microwaves stuff from the freezer section of the grocery store. If your taste buds are alive, they can discern the difference. As a man, shouldn't you be able to tell the difference between living and dead, and not gravitate to what is **dead**, what is *dying* and what will lead one to death?

The Bible says we should choose life. When we are evaluating being cursed or not cursed, we should also ask God, *"Am I dead or alive? Am I dead, or am I not-dead, spiritually speaking?"*

Being among the walking dead means most days you are vertical, but the things that are happening to you, the things you do and choose to do, may not lead to **life**. If you are sinning, that is leading to death. If you are spiritually alive you don't want to sin; you try not to sin because you want to do things that lead to life.

In very much the same way that you would childproof your house for your toddler, God has created a whole foundation to death-proof mankind. This whole planet is a foundation for us to live, move, have our being and do our purpose and purposes, but **He has instructed us to LIVE and not DIE.** God has instructed us to *choose* to live and not choose to die. The foundation that God established for us promotes life and leads to life.

We do that by accepting Jesus as our Savior and Lord. We pray, we praise, we worship, we live a fasted life, we study the Word, and *do* the Word of God. Therein lies our protections, and our **living** and our *being*. Amen.

The devil, has made traps, pits, ditches, and derailment opportunities, making the field irregular, uneven, and he is trying to lead every man to what he hopes will be death.

God is telling us to **live**, and He has set us up to live. God intended for man to live forever.

The spiritually dead, even if it was your ancestors, will take that pitted, ditched, irregular, **dead foundation** and do nothing about it, completely missing that it is wrong; not knowing that it is not in God's plan for their lives. They will try to build on it, anyway, all in their flesh they try to just make it day by day, do the best they can and hope--, *hope* that things work out. But, unless your ancestors got saved and became spiritual and handled your family's foundation problem the right way, you will still have a dead foundation.

The repetitive problems that you see in your life are evidence of foundation problems, such as a bumpy field and hindrances to success and victory in life. You need to heal your foundation, and that will take some work, but it is doable, ***with Jesus***.

We all need Jesus.

Complaining about the inequality on the playing field and doing nothing about it is the same as living a jacked-up life, not realizing it, and making it more jacked up, and then passing that jacked-up-ed-ness on to your children. What do you care? Your children? Oh, you care, if for no other reason than God will be judging you by your children. They will speak for you in Eternity. *You knew that, right?*

You don't want to continue serving these idol *gods* even if you find out who they are and what they want. They can never be appeased, if they could, don't you think 300, 500 or more years later, wouldn't the debt your ancestor "owes" them be paid off by now, if it could be paid off?

Even though we are spirit, we don't have the power to pay off an evil **spiritual** debt; we need Jesus Christ.

If you start dealing with idols, thinking you can appease them; you can't, it will sign your bloodline up with the devil, for another three, four, or more generations, further afflicting your children. So, you have to get rid of these demons/idol *gods*. **Get deliverance.** Silence them spiritually or else they will continue to afflict your bloodline. That means your children and your grandchildren, as they continue to contaminate and pollute your family's foundation and make life harder for them.

You need Jesus. Accept Him as your Lord and Savior today.

Be studious and vigilant so you don't get initiated and tricked, trapped into occultic things without realizing it because of peer pressure, cultural habits, ignorance and/or disobedience and not knowing any better because of being spiritually dead. Many get caught into devil traps by grabbing for the "free" and easy things. If it's too good to be true it is either not true, or it is ***not good***. Eyes open.

After your foundation is healed and things are going right in your life, Praise God. But don't get arrogant. Don't compare yourself with others, unless the others are in the Bible. Compare yourself with the Word of God and with what God says should be happening in your life once you are no longer oppressed by the devil.

Just look at your own work to see if you have done anything to be proud of. You must each accept the responsibilities that are yours. (Galatians 6:4 ERV)

Oh, That Flesh Life

The devil perverts the definition of what it means to be living *life*, and humans fall for it. It is so perverted that those who think they are *living*, evaluated by how much **fun** they're having are actually on the broad road that leads to death.

In the beginning was the Word, and the Word was God. The Word is part of a solid foundation. Truth is part of a solid foundation. Worship is part of a solid foundation. Dressing the Garden is man's *worship,* and it is what God sent us here to do. If you're not dressing the Garden, don't even know that there is a Garden to dress, or where it is, then you're not *living*. If you are bound up in sin, the Cherubim with the flaming sword is still at the entrance to the Garden, if you even happen to find God's Garden, how will you get in?

The purpose of your life, the entrance to your destiny, the entrance to real *living* is in that Garden of God. We need to get back into relationship and position with God. We can only get to God through Jesus Christ. We need Jesus.

The Law of God is part of the foundation. If you are not obeying the laws of God, no wonder the playing field is working against you because of the Law of Sin and Death.

God told Adam and Eve, **Don't sin, because if you do you will surely die.** Adam and Eve **died** spiritually the day they ate that fruit, and that is why we are having problems to this day, unless we have severed ourselves from that evil foundation because we are born into the bloodline of Adam & Eve. And that is how people can still walk the Earth and be spiritually dead--, kind of like zombies. It is ludicrous to enter onto the *playing field* as a spiritual zombie and expect to win victories.

I'm calling what God made in Genesis the foundation. Everything God creates is alive; the foundation lives.

Everything was in the Garden, including food. God would not create food, tell you where it is and that you can have it but not let you have it, unless you're in spiritual hospice and you don't need to eat. If you're among the spiritually dying or spiritually dead, you do not need food.

On the Seventh Day, God took His rest. We are not at rest yet. We are in the Sixth Day, the Day of Man--, we should still be working. Woe unto those who are at ease in Zion. We all need to work while it is day because when the night comes no man can work. We need to be working out our salvation with fear and trembling. We need to be working on our foundation. We need to be doing the work of an evangelist, and whatever else the Lord instructs us to do.

The foundation we inherited from our fore parents, Adam and Eve is not what God spoke, created, organized and ordered. Generations later, neither is the foundation that our kids have inherited from us because of all our ancestors' and our own sin. Because of our own forays out into the world, because of our *adventures*, and rebellion in our own version of *living,* we too have added to the pollution in our own family's foundation.

What we believed was living was not living at all, unless it was Godly and led to **more life**, spiritually speaking. Anything that leads to death is dying. Sinning is not living; it is dying because it leads to death via the Law of Sin and Death.

First Things First

The foundation is for life, it is for spiritual things, for salvation and redemption. We think of foundation as what is beneath, but it can also be what is **first**, what is primary, what is necessary and essential. Sin destroys foundations. The laws of God are integral parts of the foundation to our being, existence and survival, both physically and spiritually. When we violate them, we chop at the foundation that God put in place for our life, godliness, protection and spiritual survival.

If the foundations are destroyed what can the righteous do? The Law is foundational to Grace. If the Law is done away with what becomes of Grace and those who are enrobed and draped in Grace?

By Grace, we are saved. Because no one can keep the Law, we who are alive, are alive by Grace, and by the Mercy of God.

When God smites, He smites. But when there is a Grace period between sin and physical death, we should be thankful. God allows us to be vertical the next day and the next, so we have a chance to **repent** and come to Him or come back to Him if we are backslidden. He does not desire that one would be lost. Not one.

Abraham's obedience was accounted to him as righteousness. Abraham's righteousness was also deeded to his generations. Abraham tithed in Levi. That means that the good that a man does transcends into his generations as well. There are rewards for obeying the Law, such as honor, respect, a good name; it was accounted unto Abraham for righteousness. All that is foundational and creates favorable playing fields.

Our foundations, as it pertains to our children, has both good and bad in it. There was stuff that we received that was wrong when we got it and if we didn't notice, didn't care, didn't do anything about it, then we passed on that same **faulty foundation,** or worse, to our children, whether we suffered through it ourselves, or we did the sin that caused the problems, the children pay the price.

It's natural that we don't want our kids to have to go through or suffer through the stuff that we had to struggle with in life. So, we choose to, and try to make it better for them, if we love them. Usually, by doing natural, and obvious things for their comfort and convenience. That's not foundation building. That is only flesh-building.

Parents, it is your first job to level the playing field for your child, even and especially if it was not level for you. This must be done *spiritually*.

Everything that you came up against and everything that came up against you was not **the man**, the system, racism, ageism, sexism, or any kind of *–ism*. If you only see the *-isms*, you are only seeing the obvious and not looking any deeper. It is the collision of the *spirits* in the people you meet and their response to the *spirit* or *spirits* in you that cause the manifestations of hate, disappointment, failure, loss, et cetera.

We should make things right spiritually for our children even before we get pregnant. We should be working on it, even while pregnant. As soon as we deliver, it is not over. It is an ongoing process.

If no one did it for you, do it yourself, for yourself. Then do it for your children; do it for your family. You must get rid of spiritual things that make people hate you. If there is a *spirit of reproach* on you, if the person assigned to hate you has no spiritual depth and cannot understand that there is no reason to hate you, you do the **spiritual** work and get that *spirit* off you! Find out why that *spirit* is in your life. It is part of the Curse of the Law. Now, solve it, spiritually.

Disfavor is a *spirit*. Rejection, also. Get rid of the *spirit* that makes people choose others over you. Hindered progress: why can't you get *your chance*? As I said, you don't just murmur and complain and blame it on the privileged. You don't just blame it on flesh and blood, even though our history books are filled with stories of that, accompanied by many bloody wars.

You do something about it, spiritually. The Bible is filled with stories of *that*! God will deliver you and make you irresistible, even to your enemies. They will favor you if God favors you. The Lord can make your enemies be at peace with you.

Anything ungodly in you or on you, that remains, gets into the bloodline. It gets into the blood and is passed into your generations. This means that your foundation is corrupted. This means that you cannot have a level playing field in life because it will be built on an unlevel foundation, And, neither will your kids nor grandchildren.

Favor can get in the bloodline too. That's how a grandfather, a father and a son are blessed, generation after generation. Ask God to let that be your case.

Are any of these patterns in your family? Nobody finishes school/education. Nobody gets or keeps a job. Nobody gets married. Nobody *stays* married. Wayward kids? Where are your kids? Are your kids even, okay? How are your finances? We realize these problems in the natural world because in the flesh is where we feel it. But, know what is happening in the natural has its roots in the spiritual world.

Some of the reasons for the above problems could be anything from evil garments/filthy garments, evil petition, evil verdicts, evil handwriting, to hijacked destiny clock, a buried star, covering cast, *spirit spouse*, hijacked star, evil calendar, counterfeit scroll, evil load, **exchanged destiny, or exchanged star.**

Whatever the problem, whatever the cause, know that all of these problems are curses. Whether they came as the Curse of the Law from outright sinning, or if they were manipulated by witchcraft. If the curse was sent to curse you it would never have alighted unless there was a cause for it to alight – that is unrepented sin on your part.

In the Book of Numbers, God would not allow a curse to alight on all of Israel because God had blessed them and therefore, they could not be cursed. Shouldn't that also be your case?

But if a curse is allowed to alight--, doesn't matter how it got there; if it's on you, it's on you.

Do you think Chad knows anything about this, spiritually speaking, or how to help you get free of it? Of course not. Crying to the human person who is or appears financially successful can only go so far. Crying in the natural *against* the human who *is* successful, comparing your situation to theirs--, God sees that as murmuring and complaining.

When you say that Chad created this problem – Chad is not your ancestor and *Chad* was not tempting your ancestor 500 years ago to sin. Perhaps there was desperation in your bloodline even if created by other humans, we won't deny that as a possibility, because some humans are evil. But, the choice to live and seek God, versus the choice to sin and choose *not*-life and ask a demon or an idol *god* should have been presented to your ancestor – if that culture even knew about God. If someone in Chad's bloodline had something to do with the temptation and or sin of someone in your bloodline – we do not war against flesh and blood. You still must handle this whole problem in the Spirit.

Looking to the man that is advantaged or privileged and asking him to bring you up to where he is, or up to where you want to be without acknowledging **God**, could be what caused your bloodline to get into this situation in the first place, and caused the creation of the foundation that you were born into.

Unsaved Chad and Sharon, like you, will only react to what is presented to them. If you are saved, then you are expected and obligated to behave differently.

So why don't people help you instead of running you down? It's because this is spiritual, and the devil is in it. People who treat you badly are not (usually) Godly.

Look deeply, not just at the obvious, Are you even going to the right place and right people for help? You don't go to a manicurist for a foot operation. The manicurist looks at the **surface**, the obvious. A foot surgeon looks deeper into the foot to try to correct the problem, in the physical.

Warning: The occultic man, though he is spiritual, may seek an answer but stops short of God and lands in the 2nd heaven where he gets psychic and New Age information. These types don't offer deliverance; they offer the semblance of relief. The second heaven type acts as a middleman and is looking for what is in it for him as he or she "fake" helps you.

The spiritual man of God looks *past* the foot into **all dimensions** and asks, *What happened here?* The spiritual man of God seeks in the Third Heaven, where God sits, where God rules and reigns. That real, spiritual person doesn't let go until he gets the answer from **God**, via the Holy Spirit. Further, the Godly person does not try to profit off your mistake, mishap, or need for deliverance. Make sure you're going to the right person to get your solutions.

We all need Jesus.

We must present ourselves to God as a living sacrifice so He can help us get right with Him. Your corporate boss most likely doesn't do deliverance.

Maybe he can, but most likely not; so no need to run to him. So why do people run away from God? Why do they run away from real church, when that is exactly what they need?

When a person thinks money is the answer, he will seek a man with money. If only he could see his problem as more than the obvious, but deeper, and that it is spiritual. If he could, he will seek a spiritual answer, a spiritual person **of God** and not someone who just looks or acts the part.

Unaddressed, unfixed, the longer this stuff remains in your bloodline the deeper the roots go, and the harder it is to get rid of it. The first years of adult life may be great, and you think your family finally got past – whatever hit you in your teens or 20's. But if familial curses are time released on a satanic calendar you may have been having a wonderful life until a certain age. Pow! What happened? We don't know – but the Holy Spirit knows.

With houses, some foundation problems can be caused by the very thing that you planted to bring beauty and curb appeal to your home. **Roots of trees that have matured can destroy a foundation.** Roots are underground, unseen, and like curses can be sneaky, strangulating, and devastating. Things you did to make your life better, things you planted may backfire in time. Maybe you were tricked or didn't know any better. Perhaps there are plantations in your foundation that were allowed through the generations of your bloodline. Well, once you know, it's up to you to do something about it.

It Is Good to Repent

Repentance of individual, family, and ancestral sins, that have led to evil covenants that allowed curses, bondages, and yokes, sets you free and sets your children, future children, and grandchildren free to live and t**o have life and** have it more abundantly. Else, the same evils from your family's known or hidden past, no matter how far back, that chased you, will be chasing your children.

Free yourself and your family from the **unsaved** *Chads* that either don't owe you anything or feel that they don't owe you anything. Free yourself from the **saved** Chads who may be churched, but not spiritual, who don't even know what a spiritual problem is, or its cause.

Free yourself from the *evil* Chads who are glad that you're on the bottom and they are on the top, they are first, while you are last. Remember, Chad didn't do it. There is no way Chad could have, without divine or another type of spiritual intervention, orchestrate that everyone in a people group would be mistreated in the same evil way.

Put your entire hope in God, not in man.

Repent so that spiritual stuff you never saw, but that you only noticed that the playing field wasn't level doesn't continue in your life and foundation. This is the reason we need Jesus, and we need to pray. Stuff hidden in your foundation, jacking it up, and not to level it, instead, blowing it up, making sink holes, potholes, pits, and ditches in it, covering it, burying it so it makes you work twice as hard as everyone else, is why we should be quick to repent, for both ourselves and our ancestors. Repent, so God can heal your foundation and you can get to level ground, spiritually. Once the spiritual is corrected, favor and good success will follow in the natural.

Outside of Time

Your ancestors' demons are still pursuing you. <u>Why</u>? Because they *can,* or because they think they can. Your ancestors made spiritual deals **outside of Time.** They did this by making future promises without even realizing it, or caring. Know this: **Time** is a ***dimension*** that we have access to. We are responsible for what we do in the dimension of Time because we are *spirits*.

Sharon, you remember her, *right*? She paid you back for mistreating her, and she did it *outside of time* because witchcraft does that. That's why the dimension of time needs to be addressed when praying against witchcraft and curses that have landed on your life **and** in your bloodline. That's how witchcraft curses keep happening even after ancestors are gone. Those evil **altars** are still hurling curses against the people in your family line unless repentance to God has been made and accepted by the Lord God. **Curses are not limited by time.**

How do we get out of this mess? How do we stop these curses? **Seek Jesus**. Get saved. Repent. Renounce the sins; repent for all your ancestors. Break evil covenants down your family line. Break every curse that is a result of the evil covenant. Bind every demon sent to enforce the curse. Break familial yokes, break bondages. It takes so much more to get out of the results of sin than it takes to get into it. This is one of the main reasons why you **MUST** pray. Praying also transcends Time.

Back in Genesis, God created our Earthly foundation, set order, brought things into being, got rid of things that needed to go, by *speaking*. We are created in God's image and likeness, so we also speak. Hear the authority in this truth: **God speaks; we speak.** To have an abundant life we only have to speak. How hard is that?

Prayer is speaking.

Talking to God, listening to God, making decrees, declarations and proclamations to the entities who must hear your position on any given matter, stating clearly and affirmatively what you will do, what you won't do, what they are not allowed to do based on Scripture, based on who **you are** in Christ, is prayer. It is simply *speaking*. But speaking from the heart, in faith, with intent.

Prayer Is Not a Question

PRAYER IS NOT A QUESTION, IT IS THE ANSWER.

Our Father said, that while you are yet praying, He will answer. He's waiting to hear from you, in prayer. Like life, prayer is spiritual; it is *in time* and outside of time at the same time. It is multi-dimensional. It is eternal.

Your life should be filled with prayer and prayers. Your life should **become** Prayer. You should become prayer. Your words should mean so much to you and God that you know that when you open your mouth, things will happen. When you reach that point, you are now prophesying, you are being used of God as a prophet because you talk to God and hear from God daily.

This is why in His Passion, like a lamb going to slaughter, Jesus opened not His mouth, because **everything Jesus said had impact.** Jesus didn't mess around with words because **He is** the **Word.** When you speak, things happen either right away or later--, eventually, but things happen. There should be so much Word in you and so much Word coming out of you that you become--, *word*. Jesus is King of kings, Lord of lords, can He not also be Word of *words*?

Jesus did not murmur and complain as He went through the ultimate for *us*. Do you think the playing field was level for Jesus, **WHO HAD NOT SINNED AND KNEW NO SIN**, but had to allow the devil and the devils in all those Pharisees, Sadducees, and Sanhedrin Council to smirk, gloat, and boast as they thought they were defeating Him? The torture, ridicule the humiliation, pain, sorrow and horror of the Cross –, Jesus took it for you and for me for our redemption from Sin & Death. Yet He did not murmur and complain.

We owe Jesus. We owe Him service. We owe Him gratitude, praise, worship & honor.

When you open your mouth while going *through*, an undisciplined, unsaved, ungodly, carnal mouth of flesh will say something that probably should not be said—not to Chad, not to Sharon, not to anyone. You'd be amazed, even appalled at the *ears* that are listening, even when you **think** you're alone.

Jesus had the discipline and the control, as He was showing us how to go through persecutions, pain, intercessions, substitutions, standing in the gap for others; speak only when necessary and speak the Word, this way you do not set off any traps established in the Spirit against you by the devil.

What Did You Say?

Is the playing field of your life all funky and wonky because you haven't *spoken* to it? You haven't spoken to the mountain? You haven't spoken to the dry things, the dead things; have you not also cursed the dead fig tree? Standing at the dead tree waiting for fruit? It won't happen. Going to dead places and expecting to meet people who will improve your life? It won't happen.

Have you also not spoken to the stony ground, the fallow ground? Your foundation determines the soil of your life.

The purpose of praying is to talk to God, ask God a question, but the basis of the question is in the Scripture that you are standing on for the answer. Therefore, that Scripture **is** your answer. SPEAK IT. Declare it. Decree it. If you do not **speak** what you want in your life, in Christ, you will get haphazard things that you may randomly say, or that others say, the evil that has been preprogrammed into your bloodline as iniquity, or you get nothing at all.

Your life is connected to and representing your bloodline; it is spiritual. Your life should be better than your ancestors'. It should not be *life, status quo,* and certainly not **worse** than theirs. If your family is progressing, your life should not be the <u>**same**</u> life your parents or your grandparents had. In Christ you can have so much more--, so much better!

But because of your free will, you get to choose, daily. Saints of God, y**ou cannot choose DEATH and reap LIFE.** You can't choose sin and get an abundant life. You can't jump in water and stay dry. You can't go into a desert and expect to swim.

This doesn't necessarily mean that everyone else has a perfect foundation or a level playing field, but if your foundation is not right, if it is not healed, there is no way you are not spinning wheels on the "playing field" of your life. Don't waste your life, or let it be wasted for you.

I'm not saying that racism, sexism, ageism, are not real. Sexism, ageism--, any kind of discrimination--, any of the *ism's* are real. But people are influenced by idols in their lives. They take on their nature and act like their idols. In the same way an addict of food, sex, or drugs is addicted because the *spirit* or *spirits* in him want the food, drugs, alcohol, or sex. That's why there's never enough, in my case–, ice cream. Yet, an addiction is an addiction, and we must be delivered from it. I had no desire to be food-addicted, especially to be an ice-cream-aholic, but when addicted you are driven to that thing. Some *spirits* and demons have a deeper, stronger hold on people than others. Once you get that food, beverage, or sex it soothes you physically for that moment. It satisfies cravings in your soul, or satisfies that raging *spirit* in you that is having a tantrum like a two-year-old. **Today**. Right now.

Why people act the way they do and treat you the way they do is spiritual. Yell and scream at people all you want, if you haven't done the spiritual work, what's the use? The foundation will not change until you pray and ask Jesus to change it; heal it, spiritually first. That's a good question, when you pray are you asking Jesus for a spiritual solution, a soul solution or a physical solution? Could be why your prayers aren't answered as you expect. Most often we want the physical solution, because that's what we see. That is what is obvious.

Yelling, screaming, even protesting in the natural does not always make people who are doing wrong start to do right. But when we are talking about a bunch of ungodly people, they are going to do ungodly stuff. Period. Including mistreating, abusing, denying, stepping over or stepping on others. See how that's a spiritual problem, but it hurts people in the physical world where it is felt.

Why does life seem unnecessarily hard and wearisome. It's the invisible, spiritual stuff working against you. **It's the unspoken stuff that you can't hear working against you, because it was spoken so long ago before you were ever born.**

It may have been spoken by your own parents or relatives when you were a child. Word curses could have been spoken over you because that's the kind of stuff the people in your family say to their kids, and you were one of their kids.

Sharon spoke it, or *a* Sharon did it and it alighted because you did nothing to counter it, so it could. It may have been so subtle, or you were so clueless, you didn't know it was a witchcraft attack.

It was so long ago that it's forgotten, internalized. Yeah, it is invisible, but it's alive in the spirit and working--, authorized to work against you. And, if you are doing nothing about it, it will keep on working, against you. Once it is in your life, with no intention of leaving it gets in your foundation. When you have kids, it is there, waiting for them. They will inherit your problems, unless you clear the scoreboard on this *field*, the enemy will always be winning.

The reason people are not handling things in prayer is because they are **not praying**, at all, regularly, or correctly; therefore, their relationship with God shows no results. So, then they say, *Why bother?* The problem is not God, it is powerlessness because of prayerlessness. You can't expect to become powerful in prayer and because of prayer in one 5-minute, desperate prayer.

When the **praying field** is not strong with a strong foundation; when it is not level, the playing field will not be level either.

Don't give up: you can make it level. **YOU** can speak into your own life spiritually to level things. When you're in right relationship and right step with God, people will respect you, destiny helpers will arrive, people will favor you. You will be winning, ruling and dominating the field of your life. We work out our salvation with fear and trembling.

A Thousand May Fall

A thousand may fall at your right hand. I thought that meant a thousand may die, and it may mean that. But if a thousand people start school and a thousand don't complete it--, they *fell*. If a thousand people start a business and don't succeed, then they *fell*. If a thousand people get married and don't stay married, they fell. God says this thousand falling problem will not come near you. Why?

Often, we read in Scripture verses: I **WILL SAY OF THE LORD. I WILL *SAY*. I will say. I will say.** I will believe and I will say, the LORD is my Helper, I will not be afraid of what man can do. The Lord is my rampart, my refuge, my ever-present Help.

Pray: Arrows and pestilence will not affect me. You have to say it. Say it with dedication, and faith.

At some time in the past, but *outside of time* as we know, there may have already been arrows fired into your foundation transcending space and time. Prayers transcend space and time. God transcends space and time. The Word of God transcends space and time. The Word of God will perform. His Word will always perform, so that is what you pray. Like God, send the Word to heal your foundation. PRAY.

Send the Word to level your field. But you need to know where to send it.

The Earth, the foundation, the order, were set in place by God to bless mankind--, before sin. Evil has found a way to pervert the entire foundation and subvert that, since sin. Because of sin we see there was a proper spiritual foundation that was changed by Adam and Eve's choices. There is a foundation of Time; God sets certain seasons to bless His people.

Individuals have a foundation. Families each have their foundation. Areas and territories have foundations. There are as many things making a playing field unlevel as there are possible interferences in any number of the foundations that you may be subject to.

You can undergird, change, and support all good foundations in your life by **prayer**. You speak into your foundation by prayer and by worship to God and service to God's people.

Whatever your family/bloodline came here to do and how you did it or didn't do it, is what has either built or torn down your foundation. What is your family's foundation? What does your family believe in? Trust in? God will shake everything that can be shaken. If the foundation doesn't hold, it will be destroyed and must be rebuilt.

When we build on a firm foundation of Christ, we can withstand whatever comes our way (Matthew 7:24). Take heart; a faulty foundation can be repaired.

> And they shall rebuild the old ruins, they shall raise former desolations, and they shall repair the ruined cities. (Isaiah 61:4)

If my people who are called by my name, shall humble themselves, and pray, and seek my face, and turn from their wicked ways; then will I hear from heaven, and will forgive their sin, and will heal their land. (2 Chronicles 7:14)

Here is another perk of obedience; God says He will heal the land. Additionally, you have authority to speak to the land, the Earth, the foundation. More than just authority, you have responsibility actually, if you're even supposed to *be* there. We all must seek God to find out where we are supposed to be. God told Abraham and many others in the Bible where to go and where to live. God commands blessings for us in certain seasons, times, and *places*.

Territorial demons, strongmen, and principalities lord over their assigned places. We shouldn't be afraid, but many times we shouldn't even be in some of those places. Daniel was in Babylon. He was captive there and was subject to the Prince of Persia over that area. This Hebrew boy, Daniel, really should have been in Israel. This does not mean that God can't protect you wherever you are, but you need to be *aware* spiritually, and ask God, *"Where should I be--, living, working, et cetera?"*

If all good things were automatic, we would never need to pray; and we know that prayerlessness is sin, and it is good that men always pray.

When the enemy comes in like a flood, he will flood spiritual foundations, so you need to be already be prayerful. Flooding is one of the causes of foundation failure in the natural. The devil will not just send one curse at a person or a family, he sends as many as possible. He will flood a foundation with struggles, problems, and troubles. We can take that to the spirit as well. We may choose things that we think will enhance our lives, but if we don't choose wisely, we may be subverting our very foundation, if those chosen things are not of God. While trees and plants improve your home's curb appeal, some have extensive root systems.

While an immediate, demonic fix may appeal to a person such as Sharon, as she thinks it will fix her life or make it better, idol *gods* and demons require lots of attention; they want all of your time, attention and worship. If not, they will destroy you. Then, like a scourge, continue into your foundation and bloodline to consume your generations, blindsided.

The Word says you have not because you ask not, or you ask amiss. But if you do not have the foundation, the capability to have, keep and properly use what you are asking for, why would God give it to you?

Yes, the playing field is not level, and you may not win because of curses of any variety in your foundation, and because of that you may not be able to hold on to blessings from God because of a weak foundation. See how this becomes a circular problem? It is that way by the devil's strategy against mankind.

Is your foundation **secure**? Is your foundation level, so **God** can build on it? Is it sure, so what you ask God for you can receive and build on the foundation you've been presented with? Is your foundation solid so God can build *you*? Is it well established so you can build your family and your bloodline on it?

A Field Like *Theirs*?

You're working hard, but things aren't coming to you, and that seems unfair. As humans we often ask for *things*. You must be sure your foundation is mended, repaired and healed so your **field will be level, that is solid enough for God to build on.**

Are you sure you want to level your field with the world's? Is that your gauge? What pollutants have **you** added to your family's foundation? What things have you swept under the rug that you think are invisible or that no one else can see, but it has caused a giant lump, a hidden mountain covered by a carpet that is making your foundation bumpy and working against you? Do you have unrepented sin, hidden sins?

Saints of God, **just because you walked away from a sin, doesn't mean that sin is finished against you.** We all must repent. We have to renounce, denounce our sins. We have to break evil covenants, soul ties, bondages, yokes and curses, else the results of sin may still affect you and your bloodline, and your foundation with little to no regard to *Time*.

However, if a field is not level because of **sin**, yet the perpetrator has not repented, it's not too late. Your life may not be working right, that is the nudge, the reminder that there is **unrepented sin in your life and/or your bloodline**. If it's not your sin, then it's old sin from down your ancestral line.

Jesus transcends space, time, and every dimension. We are still talking about Jesus at Calvary because He is still relevant, there is no other way by which man can be saved.

Through your prayers, God will deal with the people that want to keep you down, hold you back, tempt you, slow down your progress and snatch victory from you at the last minute. When you have dealt with all matters that concern you, and Jesus has found nothing lacking, God will avenge all disobedience in your obedience. God will deal with Chad and Sharon and every *spirit* and power that influences them. All you have to do is pray, believe in faith, and wait on the Lord.

What Are You *Even* Asking For?

Counterfeit foundations are created by the devil. Counterfeit is the foundation of the unsaved who is serving the devil's purposes. It is any foundation that does not include God. We must be saved, and we must also be spiritual, else how will we see or know what a counterfeit foundation is or what it even looks like?

A satanic foundation will never prosper. The devil creates alternate and demonic timelines all the time for people; some fall for it. Don't live by an evil calendar or satanic, Egyptian calendar versus the calendar that God has for your life.

People with counterfeit foundations appear in our lives as counterfeit people. *Yeah, he looked good on paper...but once you got to know him you found out it was not as it appeared on the surface, or from a distance.* We pray that we are the Lord's elect, and that we cannot be deceived.

If you buy into a counterfeit, if you believe it, you will begin to go by a satanic clock instead of your own God-given destiny clock. The longer you are on the devil's course, the more you will create evil timelines, resulting in *You can't get there from here* scenarios for your life.

All you have to do is become aware of it, know what the Word of God says, and **speak**. Speak to the mountains in your life. Speak to the situations in your life. You speak to the things that are not properly ordered. *Speak* to the things that are not as God says they should be.

You speak to the things that are formless and void, just as God did in Genesis. If things are not peaceful, beautiful, and have a good report and virtue and love, then *speak* to those things.

Of course, you must know what the Word of God says to know whether things are lining up or not, then speak to it. All you have to do is talk. Pray. All you have to do is talk. This will level your foundation when Godly things that you have spoken come into existence.

In leveling your foundation, you level the field of your life.

There is one field in particular that God is a fan of. We all should be doing the work of an evangelist because the fields that are close to God's heart are white to harvest. There are more than 157,000 people dying every day not having heard anything about Jesus Christ. Unsaved; they are bound for Hell. Evangelistic fields are white for harvest. Care something about the *field* of soul-winning, and God will certainly care about the *field* of your life.

There are people needlessly living inferior or demonic existences; we think they are the unsaved. They certainly are. But some *are* saved. Even some who are saved think that **all you have to do is get saved**. That is a start; **that is not all there is, getting saved is not all you have to do.**

We expect God to level our playing field. Yes, He will with your permission. You have authority in Earth, so you must give your permission. With the devil you have to give your permission, unless your ancestors already gave it, ages ago, outside of time. If you don't plan to do anything about your Earthly problems, then God will think you're okay with what the devil is dishing out to you. So God will also do nothing to help you.

Your grandma probably said, *God helps those who help themselves.* God has made us *speaking spirits* who can make Heaven and Earth agree by simply **speaking**. Saying nothing is agreeing with the devil.

No worries about stage fright; we are talking to God--, at first. Then as we get bolder, we learn to decree, command, declare, with boldness. Eventually we will speak to the enemies of God, and there is a right way to do that, via the Word of God. We do not rail against dignities. We must all learn; we must all be taught. We can speak firmly and forcefully without being disrespectful.

Favor Is Not Fair

Why would you even want the *field* to be level, anyway? Is it because you think someone has more than you do? If you're a child of God, why should your life look like the **unsaved**? God has so much more for you than the devil has for his devotees. There should be so much abundance, so many blessings that there shouldn't be room enough to receive it.

Through the eyes of jealousy, the unsaved look as though they have it all. They look as though they are having successes and are ruling the field. Many times, they will go to, and have to go to all lengths to get that success, and many have or are polluting their family's foundations. **Why do you want to be like the UNSAVED? You get your blessings from and in Jesus Christ, and no other.**

Even though you eyed the worldly people's houses and some celebrity cars yesterday, now that you know **who you really are**, you should know that the blessings of God makes people rich and God adds **no sorrow** with it. No sorrow means no evil will be added to your life, future, into your bloodline, or foundation. No pollution, no corruption, no disruptions, and no evil surprises or hidden costs for your children and grandchildren because of poor choices on your part as you try to get ahead.

You've now done the spiritual work. God has delivered you completely, as He has promised. You have sought the Lord, repented, and He has answered. Hallelujah. But the field is still not level. **This time it's in your favor.** This time you have the advantage, and in the right way. You now walk in the favor of God. Favor is not fair. You have the spiritual advantage, and that computes to natural advantage.

Now, by your testimony alone you may start to see souls saved, people set free and delivered. In so doing, just sharing what the Lord has done for you, you are doing your part to correct the playing field for others. What God has done for one, He will do for others, because God does not desire that one human soul would be lost. And the fields are ripe to harvest.

Heal My Foundation Prayer

Have Mercy upon me, Lord, a sinner. If I am none of Yours, make me one of Yours, in the Name of Jesus.

I repent of every sin that has caused iniquity and corrupted my foundation, in the Name of Jesus.

Lord, break every curse that is a by-product of my sins; create in me a clean heart and cleanse me of all iniquity, in Jesus' Name.

Lord, break every curse that is a by-product of the sins of my ancestors, in the Name of Jesus.

Father, in the Name of Jesus, I repent for every sin of my ancestors all the way back to Adam and Eve on both sides of my family. Have Mercy on me Lord, and with Jesus as my Advocate I plead the Blood of Jesus as my defense.

I break every evil covenant that is allowing every inherited, hidden curse in my life, in Jesus' Name.

Let the foundation strongman assigned to enforce curses in my life, die now, by Fire, in the Name of Jesus.

Thank You Lord, for divine angelic detail to protect and keep me, in all my ways, in the Name of Jesus.

Deliver me, O Lord from the bloody man, the bloodthirsty man, and from all evil, in the Name of Jesus.

Lord, forgive my transgressions and iniquity, and favor me, in the Name of Jesus.

Lord Jesus, forgive me of every sin that I have ever sinned against You, in the Name of Jesus.

Lord Jesus, have Mercy upon me; judge my enemies, and let doors of breakthrough open to my life, in the Name of Jesus.

Holy Spirit, lay hands of Fire on my foundation and heal it, in the Name of Jesus.

Divine Fire of God enter my foundation and chase evil strangers that inhabit it away, in the Name of Jesus.

My life, receive Fire; become Fire, in the Name of Jesus. (X7 or more).

Fire of God, fall on me. Fall on my life. Fall on my foundation, and heal it, in the Name of Jesus.

Holy Ghost, give my foundation power to repel witchcraft attack, back to sender, in the Name of Jesus.

Smokescreen of protection sent by God to keep invaders away from my foundation, you are welcome here, in the Name of Jesus.

Clouds of doubt and confusion around my foundation clear away, in Jesus' Name.

Blood of Jesus, silence every blood curse in my life, from any origin, in the Name of Jesus.

Every parental or ancestral curse in my life, break, in the Name of Jesus.

Every inherited curse, every curse transferred from the womb, die, in the Name of Jesus.

Every inherited curse from my father's house, die, in the Name of Jesus.

Fire of God burn to ashes every evil curse in my life, in the Name of Jesus.

Every curse from the water, expire by Fire and by Force, in the Name of Jesus.

All foundational curses in my life, break, in the Name of Jesus.

All hidden curses in my life, die, in the Name of Jesus.

All self-imposed curses in my life, die, in the Name of Jesus.

All friendly fire, sent inadvertently, especially by blind witches, into my life and my foundation, die, in the Name of Jesus.

Character assassins that have studied my foundation to attack me, die, in Jesus' Name.

Every mouth that adds no value to my foundation, shut up, in the Name of Jesus.

Powers that hate my foundation with or without reason, you made a mistake, be silenced forever, in the Name of Jesus.

All curses sent by evil agents, human persecutors, fake friends, and evil ex's, die, in the Name of Jesus.

All curses and initiations in my life as a result of known or unknown rituals and ritualists, die, in the Name of Jesus.

Any curse issued against me by anyone living or dead; in time or outside of time, in any realm or dimension, expire in every realm, in every timeline, and in every dimension, in the Name of Jesus.

Every curse of reproach, hatred, rejection, and shame in my life, break and die, in the Name of Jesus.

Blood of Jesus, silence every blood curse, every sacrifice ever made against my foundation, in the Name of Jesus.

All evil handwriting against me and my family foundation, be blotted out by the Blood of Jesus.

Every arrow fired against my destiny, backfire, in the Name of Jesus.

I command every curse of failure at the brink of success to die, in the Name of Jesus.

Father, Lord, destroy every occult curse in my life and deliver me, in the Name of Jesus.

All evil doors that hidden curses have opened in my life, creating yokes and bondages against me, close, now by Fire, in the Name of Jesus.

Blood of Jesus, locate every hidden curse in my life and blot them out, in the Name of Jesus.

Lord, You said in 2 Chronicles 7:14, If my people, which are called by my name, shall humble themselves, and pray, and seek my face, and turn from their wicked ways; then will I hear from heaven, and will forgive their sin, and will heal their land.

Lord, heal my land; heal the land of my life. Lord, let the Earth and the womb of the Earth work in my favor, in the Name of Jesus.

Let every element You created work in my favor and never obey the voice of the enemy against me, in Jesus' Name.

Lord, heal the land beneath me, the land of my birth, the land of my dwelling place and the land of my workplace, in the Name of Jesus.

Heal the land of all bloodshed, whether due to war, hatred, evil, malice, jealousy or evil sacrifice in the Name of Jesus. Let the Blood of Jesus be a substitute and cleanse this land from all iniquity, in the Name of Jesus.

My foundation, you shall not make me stagnant in business; any blockages, come out now by Fire. Reveal yourself and die, in the Name of Jesus.

Lord, where is *my* Earth? My Garden? My Eden? Where should I be? Direct my paths. Order my steps; send me to the right place in the world where I should be, where You, Lord, have commanded the blessing, in the Name of Jesus.

Heal my land. Heal my foundation. Heal my playing field.

We all need You, Jesus. It is the only way this can be done. We need to heal our foundation; Jesus can do that. Jesus is that One.

Any evil arrows sent into my business, back to sender, in the Name of Jesus.

Lord, let my foundation be delivered of witchcraft captivity, in the Name of Jesus.

Lord, cure every sickness and disease emanating from my foundation, in the Name of Jesus.

By the power of the Only Living God, I dismantle every altar erected against me, in Jesus' Name.

By the power of the Only Living God, I dismantle every altar of sickness and disease erected against me, in the Name of Jesus.

By the power of the Only Living God, let the Balm of Gilead heal my wounds, in Jesus' Name.

Lord, send Your angels to help me break down my faulty foundation and rebuild it properly, in the Name of Jesus.

Every wicked assembly, council, or coven against my foundation, scatter, in the Name of Jesus.

Every wicked plantation placed and growing in my foundation be uprooted by your roots and destroyed by Fire, in the Name of Jesus.

Anything in me or about me that attracts failure to my foundation come out of me now, in the Name of Jesus.

Evil, false and wicked prophecies against my foundation, spoken by anyone living or dead, backfire, in the Name of Jesus.

Lord, I speak Light! Let the Light of God wash over me and my foundation, in the Name of Jesus.

Javelin of darkness used to pierce my foundation, be deflected and broken to pieces, in the Name of Jesus.

Sword of the Lord's Fire, conquer every Sword of darkness up against my foundation break to pieces, in the Name of Jesus.

Satanic rope used to tie my foundation, break to pieces, in the Name of Jesus.

Any power assigned to tear the foundation of my life apart, die, in the Name of Jesus.

Every clock, calendar or counterfeit scroll counting days to attack my foundation in the spirit, die, in the Name of Jesus.

Every stubborn witchcraft power that will not let me go and vows to destroy my foundation in the spirit, die, in the Name of Jesus.

Every wickedness masquerading as part of my foundation in the spirit, die, in the Name of Jesus.

Evil powers that expose my foundation to pollution, corruption or danger, die, Jesus' Name.

Every cauldron that holds my foundation captive, break, in the Name of Jesus.

Every evil hand planting wickedness in my foundation, wither, in the Name of Jesus.

Every evil in my foundation to make people hate me, dry up, in the Name of Jesus.

Lord, deliver me from every hidden curse and reverse the damage curses have caused in my life, back to sender, in the Name of Jesus.

Make me irresistible in my Godly relationships, in the Name of Jesus.

Every drop of evil urine or other excrement poured on my foundation in the spirit to make helpers avoid me, dry up and be of no effect. I break your power over me, my life, my destiny, my destiny helpers and my foundation, in the Name of Jesus.

Every evil waste material assigned to my foundation in the spirit to make me repulsive to people, backfire, back to sender, in Jesus' Name.

Every arrow of wickedness fired against my foundation to cause barrenness, backfire, in the Name of Jesus.

Every arrow of madness or insanity fired into my life through foundational pollution, go back to your sender, in the Name of Jesus.

Every backward arrow fired into my foundation backfire to your sender, in the Name of Jesus.

Every arrow of failure fired against my foundation to cause financial crisis, insufficiency, or lack in my life, backfire, in the Name of Jesus.

Every arrow of stagnancy fired into my foundation to keep me from prospering, backfire, in the Name of Jesus. I will prosper. I will have good successes, in the Name of Jesus.

Every arrow of marital failure fired into my foundation backfire into your own marriage, evil sender--, in the Name of Jesus.

Every arrow of hatred, reproach, and shame fired against my foundation, backfire, in the Name of Jesus.

Every arrow of barrenness or emptiness fired into my foundation to make me financially weak, backfire, in the Name of Jesus.

Satanic rodent living in my foundation causing havoc in my life, drink Holy Ghost poison, drink it, drink it, and come out and die, in the Name of Jesus.

Season of war, season of adversity and affliction come to an end in my foundation, and in my life, Jesus' Name.

Every evil inheritance of my father's house polluting and corrupting my foundation, your time is up, die, in the Name of Jesus.

Evil power my mother's house that vows my foundation shall not be level or strong, you are not my God. Die, in the Name of Jesus.

Disconnect from father's foundation; I connect with the foundation of Jesus Christ, by the Blood of Jesus. I cut the umbilical cord of my father's house, in the Name of Jesus.

Evil power of my in-laws' house and former in-laws' house that vows to wreck my foundation, get lost, get out of my sight, and die, in the Name of Jesus.

Evil power of every bitter Ex's house that vows to wreck my foundation, by the Blood of Jesus, I render you powerless against me. Get lost and get out of my life, forever, in the Name of Jesus.

Polygamous spirit affecting the foundation, die, in the Name of Jesus.

Every struggle as a result of polygamy, backfire and let me go; I'm not your candidate, in the Name of Jesus.

Marine powers assigned to initiate me through my foundation, die, in the Name of Jesus.

Marine powers that vowed to not let me go unless my foundation is destroyed, the Lord shall conquer you, and I will kill you and cut off your head. Die, and let me go, in the Name of Jesus.

Every evil hand stretched against my foundation wither to impotence, in Jesus' Name.

Every affliction targeted against me because of my foundation, die, in the Name of Jesus.

Arrow of death flung into my foundation come out, and backfire to sender, in the Name of Jesus.

Every problem loaded and layered into my foundation die, in the Name of Jesus.

Every devouring power against my foundation, your time is up die, in the Name of Jesus.

Oppressive powers weighing down my foundation, walk out of my life, and die, in the Name of Jesus.

Any evil load laid upon my foundation, catch fire roast to ashes, in the Name of Jesus.

Anointing, fall on me, in the Name of Jesus.

Anointing of success, fall on my foundation and bless me, indeed, in the Name of Jesus.

Anointing of deliverance, fall on my foundation and deliver it of every witchcraft power, in the Name of Jesus.

Spirit of prayer, come upon me by Fire, in the Name of Jesus.

Anointing that destroys works of darkness fall on my foundation may be set free, in the Name of Jesus.

Father, look into my foundation and remove what You did not deposit there, in the Name of Jesus.

Lord, lay Your Mighty Hands of deliverance upon my foundation, in the Name of Jesus.

God arise and favor me, in the Name of Jesus.

Blood of Jesus speak for me, guide me, and protect me, in the Name of Jesus.

Holy Spirit, my Paraclete, my Counselor; pray for me, in the Name of Jesus.

Holy Spirit, lay hands of deliverance on me, in the Name of Jesus.

Holy Spirit, lift me out of the depths of every darkness, in the Name of Jesus.

Angels of God, my life is available; remove all beggarly garments of poverty off my life, in the Name of Jesus.

Angels of God, my life is available, pull off the garments of untimely death on my body, in the Name of Jesus.

Counterfeit blessings, I divorce you and your owner, in the Name of Jesus.

Lord, let whatever I do in life align with the divine scroll of God for my life, in the Name of Jesus.

Lord, let fear fall upon my enemies and let them scatter, in the Name of Jesus.

Let the terror of God scatter the gathering of entities, people, and problems troubling my life, in the Name of Jesus.

The *spirit of death* and hell shall not locate me; I am not your candidate, in the Name of Jesus.

Lord, give me Wisdom to tackle issues as they arise, in the Name of Jesus.

Lord let every agreement with Satan to destroy my life, break, in the Name of Jesus.

Every household arrow of wickedness fired against me, backfire to the sender, in the Name of Jesus.

Household witchcraft, stand down. Household witchcraft, stand down. Household witchcraft, stand down or receive the wrath of God, in the Name of Jesus.

I break every generational curse holding me captive, in the Name of Jesus.

Lord, let every covenant with any *mermaid spirit* or *marine spirit* break, in the Name of Jesus.

Lord, I decree and declare that every covenant with idols of my father's house is nullified into perpetuity, in the Name of Jesus.

Let every covenant with *spirit spouse* break by the Blood of Jesus; I request a decree of divorcement from the Courts of Heaven, in the Name of Jesus.

Satanic bullets fired at me in the dream reverse and strike to death the sender, in the Name of Jesus.

I silence the *spirit of tragedy* walking about to overtake me and my family, in the Name of Jesus.

I silence every evil *monitoring spirit* reporting me to the Kingdom of darkness, in the Name of Jesus.

Lord, bowl over every enemy that insists on standing in my way of Your plan for my life, in the Name of Jesus.

Dark entities, powers, strangers, fade away and be afraid out of the close places, in the Name of Jesus

Evil verdict made in any coven of darkness and under the cover of darkness against me is nullified; let it be unto you and not unto me, in Jesus' Name.

Lord, let my breakthroughs amputated in the spirit received divine touch of miracle and restoration, in the Name of Jesus.

Lord, let every evil used to cover my glory burn to ashes, in the Name of Jesus.

Blood of Jesus, cleanse every evil mark off my body, soul, spirit, life, in the Name of Jesus.

Let the cage caging my finances shatter, utterly, in the Name of Jesus.

Lord, where my parents failed to make it in life I shall breakthrough; let it be so, in Jesus' Name.

Blood of Jesus, speak favor to my foundation, in the Name of Jesus.

Every strange battle in my life, and every power that brought it, scatter, in the Name of Jesus.

I command every ancient gate against me, my destiny, my life or foundation to burn to ashes, in the Name of Jesus.

Let every curse pronounced against me, break, be reversed, in the Name of Jesus.

My foundation, be released and set free of any evil padlock of any kind, in the Name of Jesus.

Lord, break up every evil reinforcement of the wicked against me, in the Name of Jesus.

Every serpent, scorpion and spider in my way--, die, die now, in the Name of Jesus.

Let every evil altar planning for my downfall be pulled down by the power of the Holy Ghost, in the Name of Jesus.

My God shall pull me away from every failure; He has never lost a battle, in the Name of Jesus.

Every threat to my reaching destiny, vanish, in the Name of Jesus.

My God shall shower me with testimonies of spiritual breakthroughs, in the Name of Jesus.

Holy Spirit, remove scales of ignorance and deception from my eyes, in the Name of Jesus.

Evil covenants against my destiny, break, in the Name of Jesus.

I worship You, Lord, in Spirit and in Truth, in the Name of Jesus.

Let every ancestral delay against me, expire, and the covenant that allows it, break, in the Name of Jesus.

Let the axe of God fall upon my foundation and break every evil implantation, every resident evil in my life, in the Name of Jesus.

Let any power using my name and picture to remote me, die, in the Name of Jesus.

Every problem designed to disgrace me and make me ashamed or lonely, you won't touch me; back to sender, in the Name of Jesus.

Lord, let all previous losses in the spirit be converted to gains in the physical, in Jesus' Name.

Any curse pronounced against my brain shall backfire to the sender, in the Name of Jesus.

I pull off and burn to ashes veils of darkness, every covering cast, and every cobweb spread upon my head, face, hands, legs or feet, in the Name of Jesus.

Every altar of infirmity raised to afflict me, return to sender, then catch fire and roast to ashes, in the Name of Jesus.

I decree and declare, by the power in the Blood of Jesus, my destiny shall not be buried. My destiny shall arise and shine, in the Name of Jesus.

By the power of the Only Living God, I recover one hundredfold every wasted year, month, week, day, minute and second, along with the opportunities lost in the past, in the Name of Jesus.

By the power of the Only Living God, sudden destruction shall be far away from me and my family, in the Name of Jesus.

By the power of the Only Living God, I break every vagabond or *nomadic spirit* from my foundation, in the Name of Jesus.

Lord, rain affliction on the camp of my enemies, in the Name of Jesus.

By the power of the Only Living God, every satanic prayer band organized against me must scatter, in the Name of Jesus.

Lord, let life be well with me, in the Name of Jesus.

Favor & Recovery, be my portion today, in the Name of Jesus.

Lord, let evil powers that arrest good things of my life, return what they stole from me, in the Name of Jesus.

I recover, by Fire, every good thing that hidden curses have stolen from me, in the Name of Jesus.

I recover all the joy and peace that hidden curses have stolen from my life, 7-fold, in Jesus' Name.

By the power of God, my foundation shall be healed and restored, in Jesus' Name.

By the power of the Only Living God, I command the Fire of God to consume every desert *spirit, barrenness, and waste* targeted against me, in the Name of Jesus.

By the Thunder Hammer of God, I shatter to pieces any pot cooking my destiny, in the Name of Jesus.

Every evil rope that tied me down, break to pieces, in the Name of Jesus.

I will not labor in vain but instead I will reap the fruit of my labor, in the Name of Jesus.

Every power of the wilderness keeping my soul in poverty, die, in the Name of Jesus.

Good success, pursue and locate me, in the Name of Jesus.

I seal these declarations across every realm, age, dimension, and timeline, past, present, and future, to infinity, by the Blood of Jesus and by the Holy Spirit of Promises, in the Name of Jesus.

Amen.

Other books by this author

AK: The Adventures of the Agape Kid

AMONG SOME THIEVES

Blindsided: Has the Old Man Bewitched You?

Churchzilla, T*he Wanna-Be, Supposed-to-be Bride of Christ*

Courtroom Prayers @Midnight

Demons Hate Questions

Don't Refuse Me, Lord (4 book series)

Evil Petition in the Court of Accusation

Evil Touch

The Fold (4 book series)

    The Fold (Book 1)

    Name Your Seed (Book 2)

    The Poor Attitudes of Money (Book 3)

    Do Not Orphan Your Seed

got HEALING? Verses for Life

got LOVE? Verses for Life

got money?

How to Dental Assist

Legacy

Let Me Have A Dollar's Worth

Level the Playing Field

Man Safari, *The*

Marriage Ed. *Rules of Engagement & Marriage*

Made Perfect in Love

Power Money: Nine Times the Tithe

The Power of Wealth *(forthcoming)*

Seasons of Grief

Seasons of War

The Spirit of Poverty

Triangular Power *(series)*

    Powers Above

    SUNBLOCK

    Do Not Swear by the Moon

    STARSTRUCK

Warfare Prayers Against Beauty Curses

Warfare Prayer Against Poverty

When the Devourer is Rebuked

The Wilderness Romance *(3-book series)*

    The Social Wilderness

    The Sexual Wilderness

    The Spiritual Wilderness

Journals & Devotionals by this author:

The Cool of the Day – Journal for times with God

He Hears Us, Prayer Journal in 4 different colors

I Have A Star, Dream Journal kids, teen, adult

I Have A Star, Guided Prayer Journal, Boy or Girl

J'ai une Etoile, Journal des Reves

Let Her Dream, Dream Journal in multiple colors

Men Shall Dream, Dream Journal, (blue or black)

My Favorite Prayers (multiple covers)

My Sowing Journal (in three different colors)

Tengo una Estrella, Diario de Sueños

Wise Counsel (Journal in 2 styles)

Illustrated children's books by this author:

Be the Lion (3-book series)

Big Dog (8-book series)

Do Not Say That to Me

Every Apple

Fluff the Clouds

I Love You All Over the World

Imma Dance

The Jump Rope

Kiss the Sun

The Masked Man

Not During a Pandemic

Push the Wind

Slide

Tangled Taffy

What If?

Wiggle, Wiggle; Giggle, Giggle

Worry About Yourself

You Did Not Say Goodbye to M*e*

www.ingramcontent.com/pod-product-compliance
Lightning Source LLC
Chambersburg PA
CBHW061334040426
42444CB00011B/2924